BRENTON BOOTH

Bash the Keys Until They Scream

Bash the Keys Until They Scream copyright © 2019 by Brenton Booth. Art copyright © 2019 by Robert Hansen. All rights reserved. No part of this book may be used or reproduced in any manner whatsoever without written permission except in the case of brief quotations embedded in critical articles and reviews.

First edition. Printed in the USA.

Cover by Robert Hansen
https://poems-for-all.com

ISBN: 978-1-926860-62-6

This is a work of fiction. Names, characters, businesses, places, events and incidents are either the products of the author's imagination or used in a fictitious manner. Any resemblance to actual persons, living or dead, or actual events is purely coincidental.

Epic Rites Press publications are distributed worldwide by Tree Killer Ink. For more information about *Bash the Keys Until they Scream* (and other books and publications from Epic Rites Press) please visit the Epic Rites website at www.epicrites.org.

Epic Rites: any press is only as "small" as its thinking

The author would like to thank the following journals for originally publishing some of these works: *Lummox, Red Fez, Citizens For Decent Literature, Chiron Review, Misfit Magazine, Pink Litter, Poems For All, Luciferous, Bold Monkey, Boyslut, Thunder Sandwich, Nerve Cowboy, In Between Hangovers, Beatnik Cowboy, Zombie Logic Review, The Blood Machine,* and *Tree Killer Ink.*

CONTENTS

LAUNDRY 11
WAITING ON THE BALLET 14
RIDING SKATEBOARDS IN THE AFTERNOON 16
A POEM FOR THE HOOKER THAT TOOK ALL MY CASH AND GAVE ME AN INFECTION 18
4 YEARS LATER 20
FIGHTING YEARS 22
THE LADY ACROSS THE HALLWAY 24
INTO THE NIGHT 26
GIRL IN A BOX 27
GOD AT 10AM 28
FROM THE ASHES 30
GARAGE 32
NUMBERS 33
THE NICEST WHORE I EVER MET 34
THE WRITER 36
DREAM LOVER 37
A REJECTION LETTER 38
THE GUILT 39
HE BEGAN TO TELL ME ABOUT GOD 40
THE HALLUCINATED SAINT 42

CALIFORNIA POEM	43
FATHER AND SON	44
FISH TANK	45
THE LOSER	46
LAST TOUCH	48
AN ANSWER	49
GOLDEN YEARS	50
THE YOUNG BEAUTIFUL HOOKER	51
THE ARTISTS	52
A LIFE IN ART	53
TRAINING CAMP	54
ANGEL WITH THE BLOODY FACE	56
FOR LOST FRIENDS	58
MURDER BY NUMBERS	59
LAST CALL	60
ONE TOUGH BASTARD	62
ANGEL ON THE GROUND	63
CREEK	64
MARK	65
A POEM FOR THE BLONDE ACROSS THE STREET THAT KEEPS WATCHING ME THROUGH HER WINDOW	66
THE FOG OF WAR	68

FAILURE 69

KILLERS 70

SUMMERTIME 71

THE THINGS WE DO FOR ART 72

HEARING HER 73

BAD DREAM 74

ELDORADO 75

SUNDAY MORNING THERAPY 76

KEEPING ON 78

APOLOGY 79

A STRANGE WHORE 80

FIGHTING IN THE PLAYGROUND 82

TOO GOOD TO RUIN 83

A FRIEND 84

FURTHER ON THE ROAD 85

CONFESSION 86

ANGEL OF DEATH 88

THE LAST FIGHT 99

THE TRICK 104

For Ruben and Wolfgang
for always supporting my writing

BRENTON BOOTH

Bash the Keys Until They Scream

LAUNDRY

That morning when I
went into the laundry
room an old lady
looked at me and
quickly turned
away
I said good morning
and loaded my clothes
into a machine
just before I finished
I felt a hand on my
shoulder
I turned and it was
her
she lived 2 levels
below me on 8
I had never spoken
to her before
but remembered her
because of the happy
look she always had
on her face
though she looked
really terrible
I didn't know what
to say and stood in
silence
she told me a week
earlier when she did
her laundry
she felt something
funny
she had been thinking
about a new plant she
had for the front
garden

and hadn't been paying
much attention
but when she had
the feeling she knew
something was badly
wrong
she closed her eyes
but knew she would
have to look eventually
and when she did
that is when she noticed
his body hanging by
the entry
I haven't been down
here again since. And
when you just came in
I thought he was you,
she said and began
weeping and I
hugged her
and tried to calm
her
though the truth is
at that time
she could have
been right
the only difference
between me and
him then
was poems
like this
one
they were
the difference
between life
or death
in a basement
laundry

found by a
terrified old
woman
that doesn't
even know
your
name.

WAITING ON THE BALLET

On broken sofas
on hot mornings,
        afternoons,
        nights,
in
front of TV sets,
being stabbed by
the news —
you look at the
clock
it has no compassion,
just as the phone
has forgotten too:
you can see people
walking by
through your window,
the water boils
and it's time for
another drink;
you can hear the
        wind,
        cranes,
        exhausts,
yet no sound of comfort:
you water the fading
plant in the corner
hoping to keep it alive:
hoping to notice another
sound,
painting,
ass,
anything to keep you
off the turnbuckle —
it will come,
it will come,
it will come,

they say you can't
stay down forever:
even the boxer only
has 10
and then he gets up
the loser
or
is carried away
and forgiven:
his job done.

RIDING SKATEBOARDS IN THE AFTERNOON

Daniel came to school that Monday
morning with his head shaved and
a rat's tail at the back which he had
peroxided blonde
it looked more orange than blonde
all day that day the other boys
teased him
we were in grade 4 and they called
him a fag and a sissy and kept
pushing him and tripping him
over
he cried a few times and that made
it all the more exciting for the other
boys
I'd never really spoken to him before
but that day began to
we met up after school out the front
of my house
I had told him to bring his skateboard
and we rode around on the street
neither of us were very good
but we pretended we were
and we tried to do tricks like they did
in the movies
I got the feeling he didn't want to go
home
when I mentioned his parents to
him I could see tears well up in
his eyes
and he changed the subject quickly
eventually it started to get dark
I didn't want to go back to my
house either
but I knew my mother, and I knew
I must
he tried to keep me on the street

riding with him for as long as he
could
I eventually told him I had to go
in
he looked upset
I asked him where he was going?
I don't know, he said.

A POEM FOR THE HOOKER THAT TOOK ALL MY CASH AND GAVE ME AN INFECTION

You did well baby
you got me walking
into you drunk and
suicidal and looking
for a fix
you sold me coke and
gave me some meth
(which I never do) and
of course I couldn't
screw you after that
and you started talking
and telling me how much
you liked me and took
my number and told me
you wanted to meet me
some time
and if I hadn't been so
close to the knife the past
few weeks
I would have never fallen
for it
but instead I licked your
pussy and all of your
asshole too
and left 3 hours later
down 1400 dollars with
a 2 day hangover and 15
days of antibiotics that
make me feel like a boiled
potato trying to stand in the
Aegean Sea
so thank you
I appreciate all you have
done for me

I wrote this poem on my last
50 dollar note
I am sure that makes you
happy sweetie.

4 YEARS LATER

I hadn't seen her for 4 years
and we drank cocktails in a
backstreet bar (her choice)
and talked. She told me about
this female superhero that had
mental issues and drank to
excess but still functioned well
and was quite amazing. As the
night went on we went back
to her place and kept drinking.
I noticed she was popping pills
and she told me she was taking
a lot of them now, the pills and
the alcohol were the only things
keeping her going, she had been
in hospital just 2 months ago
after another failed suicide
attempt. I then thought about
her just 4 years earlier. She was
so intelligent and good looking.
Most guys would have loved to
be with her: including me.
Though now her skin was pale
and bruised and her joints
heavily swollen from the medic-
ation and even her face really
didn't look the same.
I left her apartment shortly after.
She started saying things that
really didn't make any sense and
I didn't want to stick around to
see what would happen next.
The following day she sent me a
message accusing me of trying to
sleep with her. I just ignored it.
And really hoped that the super-

hero she told me about wasn't
a comic book character: but
actually her.

FIGHTING YEARS

We were best friends
we were both 18 and
virgins
neither of us had ever
had a girlfriend
I had a big head and
he had a head with
some of the biggest
ugliest pimples you
ever saw
we didn't want to be
like our parents—
that we knew
we were lifting lots
of weights
we thought we were
real tough guys
we'd bent both the
bench press bar and
squat bar at the gym
I liked to lift the back
of cars off the road
and hold them there
for a while
we were eager to fight
but no one wanted to
fight us
they thought we were
crazy
and we thought they
were:
with their boring, simple,
calm lives—
we had to be more
things went on like this
for another year or so

then Alex stopped training
and got a girlfriend and
didn't want to see me
anymore
soon after I stopped
training and didn't know
what to do
suicide seemed logical
we were 2 of the toughest
finally beaten
like everyone else.

THE LADY ACROSS THE HALLWAY

She was once a
successful lawyer
that was involved
in a national
scandal and lost
her mind
well that was the
rumour anyway
truth is
no one in the building
really knew her
but we would all
hear her most the
day —
everyday
yelling as if she were
in a courtroom to a
judge and jury that
never seemed to
understand
I lived across the hall
from her
I could hear her
but didn't mind
it was nothing music
couldn't fix
and she taught me a
lot of new words
the other tenants
couldn't stand her
you'd hear banging
on her door
abuse
even threats
after I lived there a
few months

they got a petition
together
to take to the building
manager
to get her either silent
or evicted
everyone signed but
me
a few days later the
noise stopped
she no longer even
made a sound
there was complete
silence
a couple of weeks
after
I saw her in the
hallway
she was heavily
sedated and looked
like a walking corpse
I said "hello" and she
whispered "hello"
nervously back and
quickly went in her
apartment and bolted
the door behind her
the silence continued
and every time I saw
her she looked worse
I moved not long after
and hoped
she did
too.

INTO THE NIGHT

Did a gram
and I don't
know how
many pills
started at
home then
went to a
strip club
and club
closed
at 8AM and
went to a
Chinese guy's
place with 3
other guys I'd
met earlier
got more drugs
and the guy
kicked us out
we walked to
my place
sat on the old
dirty balcony
with eyes like
clear seas
looking at the
day
knowing it
wouldn't last
much longer.

GIRL IN A BOX

I pass the gelatissimo
on Roslyn Street
and notice a little
girl with carefully
trimmed blonde
hair and pink
and white pyjamas
on
sitting inside a
cardboard box,
she's holding a
pair of scissors
in her little
hands
and her eyes
shine brighter
than twenty
cities at
night
tears well in
my eyes as I
look at her:
complete
without need,
as I walk away
I dream of
fitting in that
box.

GOD AT 10AM

Head pounding
wallet empty
10AM
walking the city
streets like a
beggar
saying the names
of all the beautiful
women I see
though none of them
knowing mine
or caring to
too broke for
the pie stand
or convenience store
too broke for
the diner
or McDonalds
too broke
for the brothel
or bar
remembering my
father
a strong man that
barely missed out
on professional
sports
paralysed weak
in the gutter
singing the drunken
songs of doom
and me now 30
years later
a mirror to him
the respectable
people walking past

with their clean
clothes and faces and
prams and lives
all looking away
from me
I want to tell them
this isn't just me
I am a writer
I am a poet
but the words won't
come
just the lips of my
mother
telling me I would
never do a thing
with my life
walking streets of
flames
hoping for gods or
death or love or
sex
anything to save me
I notice an old man
sitting on a step
with an open bottle
"Can I have a hit," I
say
"Fuck you," he said
and I smiled and
walked away
finally talking to
God
after all these years.

FROM THE ASHES

I am at home on the second
day of a 2 day hangover
broke and worried I might
lose my job
my boss called earlier
asking where the hell I
have been the past few
days
thinking about the 1500
dollars I spent on a hooker
and all the years I have
spent alone—
pounding away at my
already beaten will
trying my best not to
give in:
to keep the hell away from
the kitchen drawer—
problem is I can't think of
anyone that would miss
me
the hooker said she liked
me and would give me a
freebee next time she comes
to Sydney to work from
Newcastle:
it would definitely be nice
to see her again
but you can never tell with
them
I then get a message from
a girl I met 10 months
ago
I can't believe it:
maybe there are gods,
I respond: would you like

to come over?
but already know for the
first time in hours
how this night
will end.

GARAGE

Growing up my
bedroom was next
to my neighbour's
garage
he used it as a
home
his wife and kids
lived inside the
house
every Friday night
he would get drunk
and listen to music
the songs he listened
to were all ballads
about lost love
he'd listen to them
until the early hours
of the morning
you could tell when
he was really drunk
he would sing along
to the songs in a
low sad voice
back then I didn't
really know why
he was doing it
but now I understand
completely
drinking and listening
to sad songs on this
Friday night
trying to understand
like him
the love that went
away.

NUMBERS

It's 1/12/15 and I
have just moved into
a 2 bedroom apartment
in Newtown
it is 6:40PM and I sit on
my 20 year old sofa chair
watching the planes fly
into the clouds on the
small balcony
it is the first balcony I have
ever had
I always lived in crummy
apartments below street
level or small rooms
how did I get here?
how do we get anywhere?
are all our lives nothing
but numbers,
in a few weeks I will turn
37
older than Mozart ever
got—
far less of course—
still waiting for my numbers
to finally mean something.

THE NICEST WHORE I EVER MET

Wait! she said. Just let
me look at you for a
moment. You don't see
guys built like you
very often. Do you
work out?
No.
Aren't you lucky. How
old are you?
Guess.
I'd say 23.
No 27.
Really?
Yea it's my hair. When
I comb it this way I
look younger. You're
23.
That's right.
We moved to the bed.
I gave it to her.
It only lasted a few minutes.
I never go any longer when
I'm paying. I apologised.
It's OK, she said. I told
her I lived in Sydney and
I was just passing through
here on the way home. I
had a job in Sydney. Not a
great job. But enough for
the time being. I had plans.
And one day they'd get me
out of my job that I hated
so much.
I'm just passing through as
well, she said. I've been here
6 months now. And been

doing this about 5 months.
It pays better than waiting
or being a secretary. I just
save everything I make. I'm
going to travel. In 9 months
I'll be out of Australia. I hate
this country. In 9 months I'll
be in New York celebrating
New Years. It will be so great!
What about your family, I said.
My father died 2 years ago, and
my mother and sister are insane.
They blamed me for his death —
ridiculous people! I haven't had
any contact with them for a year.
I've got nothing in this country
anymore. That's why I'm travelling.
I'll start in America, then France,
Germany; I'm going everywhere.
I'm going to get away. I'm going
to get away, she said. It went
silent after that. We both just
laid on that bed next to each
other. Looking at the ceiling
and the walls.

THE WRITER

"He moved from Sydney
to New York to live like
Henry Miller and write
the great modern novel
like he did; though after
a year became a junkie
and still hasn't written
a word," she said
"Why am I not surprised!"
I said
and slid my hand
up her skirt
and told her
I would write
about this.

DREAM LOVER

I just got out of a bad
relationship, she said
as I jammed another
finger deep inside her.
I don't want another
one for a long time,
he was the man of
my dreams until things
started going wrong.
I understand. I haven't
had a serious relationship
for years, it's hard to find
a good partner, I said.
And she was blonde with
a pretty face and ten years
younger than me with no
pubic hairs and a nice full
ass. She told me her
favourite writer was
Nietzsche. She kept quoting
him. She would like to be a
philosopher one day, she
said. We then screwed in
several positions until I
came. She removed the
condom and wiped the
remaining cum off me
with some tissues. After
that we talked about
Nietzsche until the hour
was up. When I left the
brothel I realised we had
both recently lost the
partner of our dreams.

A REJECTION LETTER

The New England
Review send me a
form rejection and
I am drenched in
sweat from 7 rounds
of Thai Boxing
training
it's my 14th day of
training at a Muay
Thai camp in
Thailand
that's approximately
84 rounds
I wonder about the
people that get
acceptance letters
from them
could they
last 84 rounds under
the scorching Thailand
sun with a trainer
who is only happy
when you knock
him down
could they even hit
hard enough to knock
anyone down
anyway soon it will
be 90 rounds
and the New England
Review can keep on
taking work by writers
that never sweat
or hit hard enough
to matter.

THE GUILT

I was drunk and horny
and told him I wanted
him to suck my cock,
he smiled and we quickly
left the bar.

I came in his mouth
watching the city lights
through his apartment
window;
he knew I wouldn't suck
him and went to his toilet
and closed the door and
finished himself off.

I left before he came out:
wondering the whole time
if I had done something
wrong.

HE BEGAN TO TELL ME ABOUT GOD

Yea OK:
tell it to the 80 year old man whose wife died last week
and is now in a hospital bed with a broken neck
tell it to the supermarket cashier that didn't take a sick day in 45 years and
never got promoted
tell it to the 12 year old girl whose 42 year old uncle
raped her
tell it to the survivors of war
tell it to the nurses that watch babies die
tell it to the homeless guy that sells "The Big Issue"
magazine outside of Woolworths
tell it to the ones that have trekked Machu Picchu
tell it to the man that was beaten by his father as a
child
tell it to the tomb of Tutankhamen
tell it to the Rottweiler
tell it to the cab driver
tell it to the girl majoring in German philosophy
tell it to the clown
tell it to the prince
tell it to Hitler
tell it to the Dahlia Lama
tell it to Europa
tell it to the porn star
tell it to Tolstoy
tell it to the old woman that studies the Kmart
catalogue
tell it to bigfoot
tell it to a flying fox
tell it to the birds
tell it to the trees
tell it to a zombie
tell it to the blonde cheerleader
tell it to the farthest corner of the universe
tell it to all the animals at the zoo
tell it to anyone or anything but me:

because I don't really care.

THE HALLUCINATED SAINT

I was already drunk
and had some coke
then took a small
handful of pills
after an hour I was
so out of it
I laid in bed
(I couldn't do
anything else)
I opened Facebook
on my phone and
friended a few new
people
I sent one of them
some messages that
didn't make much
sense
about missing a friend
that killed himself
she sent some responses
that didn't make much
sense either
this went on for a
few hours until I could
do nothing but lay in
bed looking at things
that weren't there
a day later I sent her
a message apologising
for the messages
she didn't respond
and I didn't tell her
the real reason I
messaged her
was she looked so kind
in her photograph.

CALIFORNIA POEM

Laying in a bathtub in a hotel on
Powell Street San Francisco
drinking from a bottle of bourbon
and reading a book of poems
by Cendrars
and a relative of Bach is playing
on the radio
and the occasional flush of the toilet
comes from the next room
and the sound of a tram from the
street below,
laying in a bathtub in San Francisco
with no wife
    no children
    no mortgage
    no family
and nothing I'm worried about getting
stolen,
laying in a bathtub in San Francisco
the maid's making beds
the homeless begging
the wealthy eating a la carte
the actors rehearsing,
laying in a bathtub in San Francisco:
far far away.

FATHER AND SON

About a year
before my father
died he came to
my apartment in
Kings Cross
we listened to
music and drank
whiskey before
going to a bar
and drinking
more
we ended up
back at my place
at around midnight
I read him a couple
of poems and he
went silent
I got him another
drink but he didn't
want it
"I have had enough.
Pity I didn't learn
those words earlier
in life: things could
have been so
different," he said
and I went silent
and finished his
glass for him.

FISH TANK

Just after we started
going out she bought
a fish tank and three
small fish
"I have been looking
at them for a while
in the pet shop, but
never bought them
because I have been
trying to save money;
but now you are with
me, I am so happy, I
don't care about
money. I have given
them names: Gertrude,
Cecily, and Beatrice. I
want you to have
Beatrice. She is lovely
and beautiful like you,"
she said
I didn't really want a
fish and changed the
subject
over the next few months
the fish died one by
one
until there was nothing
left but an empty
fish tank
and not long after
an empty apartment
and 3 small ghosts
far wiser
than me.

THE LOSER

He was short and thin and wore glasses with the thickest lenses you ever saw. He had the walk of an old man and talked slowly like a special kid and always carried a laptop. I never had much contact with him but knew what the other boys would do to him. One day when I was walking home from school I actually saw it happening. "Leave him the fuck alone," I said, not really knowing why.
"Fuck you Robert!" they said.
"Well hit me then tough guys!"
They backed off. I had this tough reputation for no real reason. I was the strongest and fastest kid in my grade, but what they didn't know is I had lost any toughness I had years ago. "Hey thanks," said Jamie and I picked up his glasses and handed them to him. "It's a good thing these things are so big, otherwise I would have to explain to my parents a lot why I broke them."

I walked him home and spent the afternoon at his place. After that we were friends. Once word got around he was my friend the beatings pretty much stopped. Though he still got teased because he was different. And he was. Last I heard he was a software programmer for a big company making a fortune. While the rest of us worked crap jobs or no jobs and some even wished they were back in the schoolyard.

LAST TOUCH

I would give up my
arms
feet
face
and back
I would give up
this poem
the last poem
the next poem
all poems
I would give up
everything
just to have her
hold me again
and say
she loves me.

AN ANSWER

He sat on his sofa at 9AM
on a Thursday morning
watching the rain fall
through the window
he just woke from a 20
hour sleep
before that he was drunk
and doing lines off a 20
year old hooker's body
flexing his ageing muscles
and telling her he could
have been a great fighter
but now he isn't so sure:
who is he really?
has he become his dissatisfied
father
is it enough to live like this?
he opened the kitchen drawer
and looked at the knives
wondering if he will ever be
comfortable with who he
really is?
he decided to give it a chance
and closed the drawer slowly:
hoping he made the right
decision.

GOLDEN YEARS

I remember the first girl to show me her panties. I was 7 and playing in a playground. The slippery dip I was using was enclosed at the top and a couple of people could fit in there. I was with a girl I often played with that was the same age and lived just down the street from me. When I reached the top she was waiting for me and gave me a strange look then lifted her skirt, showing me her panties. I froze. She kissed me. I moved away from her as fast as I could and slid down the slide and ran all the way home without stopping or looking back: and they say age brings wisdom.

THE YOUNG BEAUTIFUL HOOKER

After we screwed she started telling
me that she was going to become an
underworld leader and control all
the crime in the city. She had read
many biographies on famous crime
bosses and knew she could do it.
And she was 19 with blue eyes and
long beautiful blonde hair and a body
that would make Venus frown.
Surely you can do something else, I
said.
No. This is my only hope, she said.
And I knew she'd never make it.

THE ARTISTS

When the poem
was as important as breath
when the dirty, ugly streets of Kings Cross
looked like paradise
when the job
was only a few hours a week to pay rent
when the line, bottle and pill
were as common as food
when money lasted
only until the following pay
when the tiny apartment
was better than a house
when the days were full of inspiration
when all my words were returned
when our bodies
were strong and free
when we would screw for hours
when you were the only one
that called me a writer
when all we had was each other
when anything seemed possible.

A LIFE IN ART

There's this
poem
I have been
trying to
write
for decades
I
guess when
I
do eventually
write
it
I will
know
it's the
end.

TRAINING CAMP

I had been drinking whiskey for
8 hours in my apartment
and it was now about 9PM
and I decided to go to a bar
I'd only just moved to Newtown
this would be my first night
out
I found the crappiest looking
bar I could and went inside
(nice looking bars always
hassle you when you're drunk:
crappy bars appreciate any
business they can get)
I ordered 2 whiskeys and was
feeling pretty good
I had been listening to music
and watching old MMA fights
most of the day
"What you celebrating pal?"
said the bartender
"I have an MMA fight in 2
weeks."
"Why are you drinking!"
"It doesn't matter. I will
walk straight through
him," I said and shadow
boxed for a few seconds
"Good luck mate," he said
and I took a seat at the table
by the door
I could hear the bartender
talking about me and laughing
with another customer
I finished my drinks and went
to the bar
the bartender had a grin on

his face
"Another drink champ?"
"You want to be part of my
training camp?"
he didn't respond
I left the bar and got a cab to
the brothel
several girls introduced
themselves
I told the skinny young blonde
with the small boobs and red
lingerie I was a poet
"You look more like a fighter,"
she said
"No I am really a poet."
"Sure. What do you write
about: beating people up and
sleeping with hookers."
"That all depends on the hooker,"
I said and followed her tiny
beautiful ass upstairs.

ANGEL WITH THE BLOODY FACE

I remember the first
time we got high
you were 31 and a
divorcee with bad
arthritis and nightmares
that wouldn't let
you go
and I was 24 and
trying to escape
my own unfortunate
history
you collapsed
hitting your head
on the coffee table
on the way
down
blood trickled across
your forehead
and your eyes were
distant
and you whispered with
a smile on your
lips
to faraway places
I held you in my
arms
talking gently
and you shared your
words with me
and your visions
I kept telling you
to come back
I don't want to.
I feel good for
the first time in
years, you said

and your face looked
10 years younger
I could see what
you were before the
hard times
had stuck like a
leech to you
I kept holding
you in my arms
as long as I could
my angel with the
bloody face
that I wasn't strong
enough
to save.

FOR LOST FRIENDS

Staring at this
page now
wondering how
we do it
how do we continue
going on
how do we keep
enough hope each
day to want to live
another day
and the answer is
not all of us can
and this poem was
written for all of those
that couldn't.

MURDER BY NUMBERS

Society's greatest gift
is crushing the
individual —
the ones with a
bounce in their
step
the ones with worthy
original thoughts in
their minds
the ones with a real
glint of fire in
their eyes,
all the things
that the bitter
unimaginative
uninspired
masses we call humanity
don't have.

LAST CALL

In Downtown Los Angeles
I stayed in a cheap hotel.
The room was tiny and had
one small window with a
view of a brick wall. The
bed was hard and tap water
made me feel ill. At about 9
on my first night the phone
rang, I thought it must have
been the front desk compla-
ining about my Visa credit
or something. "I need to see
you again Bruce," a desperate
gay sounding voice said.
"He's not here mate. I don't
even know who he is."
"Don't play games darling. I
need to see you."
"Who are you?"
"I am coming up. I am coming
up now!"
"You have the wrong number
mate."
"You fucker! I am coming up!"
he screamed into the phone
and hung up. It was my first
night in Los Angeles and I
didn't know what to expect,
but surely this was some sort
of scam. I decided I'd be ready
though. I stood next to the door
waiting for it to be kicked in
and I'd pounce on whoever
it was. The phone rang a few
more times but I just ignored
it. I stood by the door for nearly

an hour then suddenly realised
the real problem:
he wasn't trying to scam me —
he was just lonely, which I
understood perfectly. The
phone rang again and I picked
it up, put it on the bedside table
and laid down on the bed. I could
hear his voice coming through
the receiver, it sounded like a
whisper from where I was.
Over the next few hours I liste-
ned to every tender word he
said,
pretending like him:
that I wasn't alone.

ONE TOUGH BASTARD

He must have been in
his mid-eighties and I
would see him every
day badly hunched and
inching his way up
Victoria Street
it's a steep surface and
took him over an hour
to get from his apartment
building at one end of the
street to the shops at the
other end
but he'd do it without cane
or walker or wheelchair
or car
he was the toughest man in
Kings Cross
maybe the whole world
and when I stopped seeing
him
I didn't feel bad
because unlike most
he never
gave up.

ANGEL ON THE GROUND

Your first boyfriend
jumped off a cliff
and your husband
nearly killed you
I'd hate to hear
what I really did
to you
but I just want you
to know
if it wasn't for you
I wouldn't be writing
these words now
and no matter how
far away you are
you will always be
with me:
that bright shining
light
that never goes dim.

CREEK

We used to go there
after school to drink
and smoke pot
there was a road
above where we sat
we could see the cars
driving past
they couldn't see us
though
we'd stay there for
hours on the moist
dirt
smoking, drinking
and talking
when we were ready
to leave we'd find the
best looking rocks
put them in a stack
and throw them at
the passing cars
we never aimed at
trucks
they were too big
the cars were much
easier to damage
we'd stumble home
just before dark
in time for dinner
and an argument
with our parents.

MARK

His father was an alcoholic
and his mother never
cared much and all
the others cared just
about the same;
me included.
And he told me he
was lonely.
That he'd stay up all night
sometimes
unable to sleep
thinking about the loneliness.
And he read.
He was reading War and Peace.
I asked him why he was reading it?
I told him to read Hemingway,
or better still Bukowski. I quoted
a few lines. He smiled and said they
would be the kind of books for him.
And he'd try with every girl he'd meet
to make a friendship.
And he was a little overweight.
And he looked a little different.
And the girls wanted nothing to do
with him.
And he was a little different. And even
I didn't want to be his friend.
And on Tuesday morning they found
his body washed up on the rocks:
his sentence
finally
complete.

A POEM FOR THE BLONDE ACROSS THE STREET THAT KEEPS WATCHING ME THROUGH HER WINDOW

Well I am listening to
Satyagraha and have
just finished my 8th
glass of whiskey
I just thought of a
new story that I will
write later about a
cold hearted woman
with a large collection
of dicks she has been
collecting from men
for many years
that falls in love and
gets her heart broken
then gets drunk and
chokes on one of
them,
when the album
finishes I will watch
MMA for a while and
finish the rest of the
bottle
then shadow box a
bit imagining I could
have been a great
fighter
order a pizza
eat that
get a shower
take a dump
and try to write the
story;
so anyway
now you know

everything I will
be doing for the
rest of the day,
so please:
stop fucking watching
me!

THE FOG OF WAR

A few weeks before my father
died of prostate cancer my
mother visited him in hospital.
They had been separated for
twenty years by this time. She
didn't really come to see him
though, she came for something
else — she came for an apology.
She believed that her whole life
had been ruined by him and that
he still owed her. He was a heavy
drinker and never cared much
for the family life. He continued
drinking for several years after
my mother left him, then one
day he stopped. And a smile and
goodness that had been hidden
for so many years returned to his
face. Finally letting go of the tragic
death of his first wife, the brutality
of his childhood, and all the things
he wanted to do but never did.
Knowing that there was no point
living in the past anymore, he had
already wasted too many years on
that. And as he patiently told my
mother to never visit him again:
he wished he could tell her more.

FAILURE

She took my penis
in her mouth gently
and thoughtfully
as if it were something
truly great
she told me all the
time that I was one
of the special ones
others didn't realise it
yet—
but they eventually
would,
well I never ate her
pussy:
I didn't like the taste
and when we had sex
I did it like a wild beast
that was told this was
the last fuck it would
ever have
I just couldn't be what
she wanted me to be;
though what she never
realised was she wasn't
the only one that was
disappointed.

KILLERS

You want to scream
but you can't
you want to cry
but your ability has gone
you want to kill
but that would make you
just like them.

SUMMERTIME

Hot summer afternoons
in the suburbs
of Sydney
1980's
where even the breeze
didn't reach,
laying on my bed sweating
in my boiling room
listening to the radio
with nothing else to do;
my father at the pub
drinking
my mother in the
backyard crying:
all of us hoping for
something more.

THE THINGS WE DO FOR ART

I got a call on my radio to go
to the liquor store on level one,
it was being robbed.
Sure enough when I arrived there
was a black woman that looked
more like a big fat male wrestler:
only uglier. She had a large butcher
knife in her hand that appeared to
have dried blood on it. The sales
attendant was crying behind the counter.
"I'll kill you rent-a-cop!"
"Take it easy," I said keeping a
good distance.
Two police then ran towards us
screaming at her.
They found razors in her hair and up
her cunt. She was a real psycho.
That same week another guard was
bashed by a gang walking to his
car after a shift. My opposite was
shot in the foot. I quit a few days
later. A shopping centre is no place
to die: well not for minimum wage
anyway.

HEARING HER

She mistook me for
Van Gogh and told
me
I was the only man
she enjoyed having
sex with at work
and
the reason she never
called me was her
phone was lost
it was lucky I came
back
or she would have
never seen me
again
and she would like
to see me again
next weekend would
be good
she said
that would be unreal
I said
and left the brothel
with both ears still
intact.

BAD DREAM

She slept with a
rosary under her
pillow and always
woke up with a
fright,
I did my best to
be nice to her
and help her
out of it
over our time
together —
but it never
worked;
she'd always
wake up
terrified
then see me
and smile
and relax
and I wonder
now how many
women out there
are the same as her
waking each morning
to the terror of what
lay next to them.

ELDORADO

I have holes in my stomach
and holes in my mind—
apparently the ones
in my stomach will
heal: the surgeon
told me last week—
and the rain falls
to the beat of the
frantic cars sliding
along the tired roads
while the elevator opens
and I can hear my
neighbour's front door
slam and I am happy that
it is shut—
laying in bed on a Thursday
afternoon;
with the windows closed,
blinds closed,
lights off,
and phone off:
reading Voltaire and
thinking about Eldorado.

SUNDAY MORNING THERAPY

My son committed
suicide a month
ago
she said
and
I jammed three
fingers inside
her pussy
you're a
naughty boy
look at
that cock
it's so hard
it's pointing
at the moon
let me have
some of this
first
she said
and took a
hit of crystal
meth from
a small glass
pipe
do you want
some?
OK
I said
and had a
hit
I was already
really drunk
and hadn't
done meth
for years
I laid back

on the bed
overwhelmed
my cock was
still up though
I felt her
sticking it in
her pussy
it felt strange
everything did
the whole world
was suddenly
new
I started fucking
her as hard as
I could from
underneath
and quickly
forgot about
her son
and everything
else that was
wrong.

KEEPING ON

His father
had died
a few
days earlier
and
we sat
on his
sofa doing
long lines
and
talking about
fighting,
he told
me he
was glad
I was
there.
Me too,
I said.

APOLOGY

Forgive me Dostoyevsky
forgive me invisible man on the moon
forgive me shadows that won't pass
forgive me barking dog in the terrace across the street
forgive me dirty white car that never moves
forgive me 23 year old dictionary
forgive me sexy French neighbour
forgive me dying plants on the balcony
forgive me dusty statue in the corner
forgive me small hole in the ceiling
forgive me Dali
forgive me Hemingway
forgive me father
forgive me mother that I never see
forgive me everyone
and everything
for I am crying
now
and don't know if
I will ever stop.

A STRANGE WHORE

After I finished
there was
still 20
minutes left,
she asked me
if I wanted
to go
or
if I'd like
a massage.
I laid face
down on the
flimsy bed
and she positioned
herself on
my back —
she then picked
a blackhead I had
on my neck, then
another, and
another.
The bell rang
but she kept
on going for
about another
20 minutes.
She told me that
she'd give me $50
off next time I
came for letting
her burst them.
We dressed and
she led me out
the back exit
onto Kellet Street.
It was now 6AM

1/1/06
the sun was shining
and I felt sick.
As I walked back
to my apartment
I passed a guy
who screamed:
"This is the worst
New Years of my
life." I reached
my apartment
went inside
laid in bed
and hoped for sleep.

FIGHTING IN THE PLAYGROUND

When I was young I had bad teeth.
A few kids at school would regularly
tease me about it. They'd call me
"Dracula." I actually liked Dracula
but was always insulted because I
felt obliged to be. You know, personal
honour, etc. So I would fight these kids
every lunch. And sometimes after
school. I was tough when it was
one on one. Yet they would often
gang up on me with five or six to
one. I had no friends. So I was on
my own. The teachers all turned a
blind eye when they gang bashed
me. I eventually got braces and
my teeth were normal. We quickly
found other things to fight about
though.

TOO GOOD TO RUIN

She was asleep on my bed and I slid a finger inside her. It felt strange. I then looked at it and noticed it was in her ass. I wiggled it around a bit though she didn't respond. She was fast asleep. She slept with her thumb in her mouth. She looked so peaceful. So lovely. Like a princess from a fairy tale. I took the finger out and forgot about sex. Just looking at her asleep on my bed. Breathing her gentle little breaths was enough.

A FRIEND

I turn on my phone at 4PM
there is 5 missed calls and
a message all from the same
number
I just woke from a 2 hour
sleep dreaming about getting
eaten by a giant cockroach in
white sneakers
before that I spent 20 hours
drinking and doing coke at
several bars, a strip club, and
finally a brothel
I liked the girl so much I got
her to come home with me
the problem was when she
left and the booze and coke
wore off and I realised I had
spent 2 weeks pay and had a
hangover that could knock
out an apartment block:
things couldn't get much
worse,
I checked the message
it was from Buz
I played it
"How you doing you crazy
bastard. You left 15 messages
on my phone last night. I bet
you feel great! Give me a call
to let me know you are still alive."

FURTHER ON THE ROAD

Falling
standing
walking the long plank
trying not to see the
burning ground
underneath
hiding from mirrors
whenever possible
hoping there is something
still left
to give.

CONFESSION

He told me
he was going
to kill himself
and a friend
gave him a
copy of my
book
he didn't
want it
he never read
books—
especially books
of poetry
but his friend
persisted
he read it at
1AM on a bad
night to try to
take his mind
off things
he read it
over and over
and called his
mother the
next morning
for the first
time in 4 years
she didn't
recognise his
voice at first
and they ended
up talking for
hours
I thought my
life was terrible.
That I was the

only one. Then
I read your poems.
And realised I
wasn't the only
one. Thank you,
he said.
No. Thank you,
I said and hoped
to one day feel
the same.

ANGEL OF DEATH

I was sitting at a table in the corner of the old sports bar on Darlinghurst Street drinking bourbon and trying to forget—yesterday, last week, my whole life. Earlier I had been attempting to analyse some of my previous mistakes and come up with some sort of plan, to make things work a bit better in the future. I quickly gave up on that one, who was I trying to kid?

The bourbon was now doing its job. It attacked the senses like ravenous beasts on a fresh corpse, taking away all that I didn't currently need—which was everything. Bourbon was my good friend. He's been there for me since I was 13 and has never let me down. When I was drinking things always seemed like they were getting better. It was the perfect elixir—the true potion of the gods. The only thing that ruined it is when you stopped drinking, and it's impossible not to sooner or later. The body eventually wants a meal, a sleep: some fresh air. And that's when the problems start up again.

It was a hot Wednesday night in Kings Cross. The air was thin and choking everybody, all our heads were spinning through lack of oxygen and everyone was full of life, the dark skinned doormen at the pubs and clubs were looking for arguments and fights, the taxi drivers turned down crap fares and honked their horns as if necessary, filling the sky with a never ending bleak toneless symphony, the hookers wore gloves and bikini tops and miniskirts and six inch clear heels, with freshly bleached golden hair catching guys like cheap bait dangling in front of a baby fish, junkies sat drugged in hidden corners—higher than constellations, booze and conscious wrecked men in suits stumbled home to their crumbling families, tired police cautiously walked along the strip—hoping for a quiet night, teenagers tried to hustle drugs and beer and talked tough to the hookers, and naive tourists with stars in their eyes photographed the huge Coke sign and all the neon clubs, dressed in their finest, hoping for a night to remember.

I was sitting alone. I was a regular at the sports bar. No one ever bothered me. I really didn't look like the kind of guy you'd want to bother. I stood 5'11, weighed over 200 pounds, with a flat stomach and arms full of tattoos, covering the muscles that stretched my skin. When I was younger I was always the strongest and most athletic kid at school. I never did anything with it though. I never had any desire to do anything worthwhile—broken families do that to people. Occasionally I went to the mixed martial arts gym now and did some training. It was great. Getting beat up by 20 year olds on steroids, or even sometimes beating them really made me feel good. I loved it there: something was happening, not much—but something.

I stood up and went to the bar and got a couple more glasses of bourbon. After that I returned to my small table and left the drinks there. I then headed to the toilet. Standing at the urinal I noticed some freshly written graffiti. Apparently there was a new guy in town called Steve, who had a big dick, and wasn't greedy with it. A mobile number was scribbled at the bottom of the message.

I saw a girl sitting at my table as I approached it. She was a natural blonde with dark slacks and a light-blue long sleeve top on. She looked out of place. You didn't normally see girls at this bar at all. Though you rarely ever saw them with so much clothing on this street. "Excuse me darling, but you are sitting at my table," I said and she turned and gave me a thorough examination with unmistakably sad looking eyes. She was really taking her time responding. Looking at her carefully I realised she had a serious body on her, though her face was worn and weary. She tried to hide it under carefully applied make-up. It didn't work though, how could it? It was her soul that was battered—not her skin.

"I'm sorry. All the other tables are full. Do you mind if I sit here for a while. I promise I won't annoy you," she said.

"I have never trusted promises. Though I don't mind if you sit here."

"My name is Liz."

"I'm Robert."

"You look like a football player. Are you a football player?"

"You got the wrong guy. Nothing special about me baby."

"You and everybody else."

"What are you drinking?"

"Vodka and lemonade."

I went to the bar and ordered Liz a drink. Shortly after I returned with the drink and gave it to her. I sat and drained one of my two glasses of bourbon.

"You scared of alcohol or something?" I said.

"I really shouldn't be drinking tonight."

"Why not?"

"It's a long story."

"I don't have anything else to do right now."

Liz gave me a long pensive look.

"Alright," she said, "you really want to know more about me. Well I work down the street at Pinups. You know the place?"

"Yea it's that overpriced strip club."

"I guess you could call it that. Anyway I called in sick tonight."

"What's that got to do with you not drinking?"

"Well the place is run by the mafia. And if one of my bosses sees me here drinking—I'm in serious trouble."

I didn't respond. I just looked at her while I worked away at my glass. She was starting to sound like my kind of girl. As I was looking at her I noticed a change on her face, like she was relaxing a little. She then excused herself and went to the ladies. I drained the rest of the glass then turned my head in her direction. When I did she was looking back at me from the entrance to the toilets. I got up and ordered more drinks.

She was completely different when she returned from the ladies.

"Did something happen?" I said.

"One of my bosses just saw me."

"The mafia guy?"

"Yea."

"Did he say anything?"

"No he didn't. That is what is scaring me. I better go. I was just really tired and didn't want to work tonight. Though I don't have a choice now. Those guys are really not good to get on the wrong side of."

"Hey screw that! You are with me right now. And no one is doing anything to you while you are with me. I don't give a fuck who they are."

Liz gave me a long piercing look. Then picked up her glass and drank it in one hit.

"So you are a real man," she said.

We both stumbled along Bayswater Road—well I was stumbling, Liz was continually falling: luckily even in the state I was in my reflexes were sharp enough to catch her, and save her from the ugly reality of the asphalt footpath. Several hours had passed. It was just past 3AM and we'd recently been kicked out of the sports bar.

"You're too drunk," said Charlie the doorman.

"One can never be too drunk. Not in this world anyway," I said.

Charlie didn't quite understand the whole philosophy behind the statement. I didn't resist his request though. He was a good guy. We'd occasionally have drinks when he wasn't working, and sometimes trained together at the mixed martial arts gym. I generally preferred not to train with him. He was a Kiwi with a body like a Mack Truck. It wouldn't have been his call anyway. The new bar manager must have asked him to kick us out. He's only been in charge a few weeks now and thought he knew it all. Give him a few more, and he'd learn his place, I thought to myself. It wasn't so bad though. I had Liz. She was some woman. She talked about depression, broken family, failed loves, failed dreams, working crap jobs, and the occasional thought of suicide—she was definitely my kind of girl. And to top it off, she had a body you wouldn't believe. Charlie gave me a big pat on the back and a wry smile as we left the bar.

"Why did he do that for?" said Liz.

"Cause we are good friends" I said.

"I sure hope so. Cause if you think you just scored with me, I am not that kind of girl."

"I know baby. You are a real lady—one of the rare ones. And I'd never do anything to disrespect you."

"Now that's better."

We continued along Bayswater Road to her apartment. She was getting worse and worse. I was basically holding her up now. There was no one much around. It was nearly a deserted street, apart from a couple of other drunks kissing and a few junkies crashed out in doorways. "I want to stop here and rest a minute," said Liz, out the front of Bayswater Bistro. There were half a dozen black and white tiled steps that led up to the restaurant. I lowered her onto one of the steps and began kissing her. She responded eagerly. I worked a hand into her pants, past her panties and slid in a finger. It went in without any resistance—she was dripping wet. Liz let out a loud moan. I continued working it around in there.

"We can't do this here. There's people around," said Liz.

"There's no one around," I said while mounting her.

"What about them," she said pointing behind me.

I turned around and saw a couple of teenage boys standing a few feet away from us with sheepish grins on their faces. I couldn't believe it. "Is there a problem?" I said standing up and moving towards them. They both quickly walked off into the darkness in silence. Liz stood up.

"I'm sorry," I said.

"It's OK. The looks on their faces when you stood up and spoke to them were hilarious. They were terrified! Come here tough guy," she said kissing me and sliding a hand in my pants.

We continued along. Eventually reaching the gate to her building. It was strange. Most buildings in this area were on the street. Hers was back from the street in a large courtyard surrounded by other buildings and exotic looking trees. I'd lived in the area for ten years and never even knew that her building existed, that's how well concealed it was. Passing through that gate was like entering another world. You could probably do anything in there, and nobody on the outside would know about it.

We eventually made it up the three flights of stairs to her apartment. It was a one bedroom with four windows that looked at a brick wall. It was pretty grim in there, wouldn't get much natural light. Liz excused herself and stumbled off to the bathroom. I had a look around the lounge room. She had an impressive sound system. Above which was a large reproduction of a Bosch painting—full of devils and nudes and death and sex. I looked through a few of her CD's and found Black Sabbath's "Paranoid." I put it on and turned it up to a good volume. I was feeling pretty good. I found a bottle of bourbon in the kitchen and poured two highball glasses—putting more in hers of course. She was some girl and this was some place. A girl like this could really shake up a guy's life, I thought to myself.

It seemed like she had been gone forever. I went to the bathroom door and knocked. "Hey baby, when you going to come out—I miss you," I said. The door then opened and there she was. I grabbed her hard and kissed her greedily while lifting off her top. I had problems with the bra. It just wouldn't seem to come off for some reason. After a minute or so of fumbling around she gently pushed me back and took it off herself. She seemed to have sobered up a little, well her coordination had improved slightly anyway. I started licking her tits—she had the good ones with the big nipples. After my tongue worked them a little they both stood up like proud guards ready for anything. "You like Black Sabbath," said Liz as I worked my hand into her panties. I nodded. She led me into the lounge room and sat me down on the sofa. She removed her pants. She was now in a skimpy black G-string and brown cowboy boots. She began moving around the room. Doing a drunken, obscene rendition of a well-rehearsed dance of hers. She was all sex this girl. And had the best ass I had ever seen.

She eventually worked her way back to me. Thrusting her panties against my face. I pulled them off violently and began tonguing her thing. It was light pink and tasted good. I started working on her clit. She let out some moans. I kept going as if possessed. She got hotter and hotter. She was about to cum and went to move away. I held onto her with all my strength. Soon after she let out a really loud dirty moan: no, it was actually more of a scream. The whole building must have heard it.

When she finished she kissed me then pulled off my shirt and pants and underpants and started working on me. She was no virgin that was for sure. She took that thing like an old hand with those expert lips. It was really something. I could hardly believe it. A strange thing was happening though. It was really odd, maybe I'd drank too much, it didn't normally effect me this way though. Regardless my cock wasn't really responding. It just lay there like a corpse, that wants nothing but rest. She continued working away though completely unfazed. I sat there watching her head and mouth work and work, to no avail. It was starting to get embarrassing. "Stop it," I said calmly. She kept going as if oblivious. "I said, STOP IT!" I said angrily pushing her face away. I must have hurt her. It looked like I'd hurt her neck when I pushed her. "Why did you do that, asshole! It's not my fault you can't get it up," she said with an expression on her face that infuriated me. I looked at her intensely for a moment. She sure had some body. But the body couldn't hide her face that housed a soul that had been torn again and again. She had such a weathered face. Who the fuck did she think she was? I lost control at that point. I stood up and slapped her hard across that weathered face. She screamed and fell. I then kicked her a couple of times in the stomach when she was cowering on her hands and knees on the floor. She didn't make another sound.

She was bleeding from the mouth and nose and sprawled out on the lounge room floor when I left.

I awoke the following afternoon on the floor of my bathroom beside a neat pile of vomit. I cursed and slowly stood. I looked at myself in the mirror. My face appeared like it had gone a hundred rounds against Jim Beam and lost. I looked truly terrible. I could smell a strong aroma of pussy on my lips then remembered Liz. "Fuck! What did I do? I have to be some sort of complete fucking asshole to have done that to her. Why? Why? Why? "I thought. It felt like a ton of bricks had landed on my conscience, busted straight through the foundations, and fallen directly where guilt lived.

I found a small piece of paper with her name and number messily written on it in my pocket. I thought about calling it to see if she was OK. I agonised over it for a while. Problem was if I did, I might end up in jail. And that was somewhere I really didn't want to go. The thing was, I wasn't sure if I'd given her my number or not. If I hadn't I might be safe. I couldn't remember giving it to her. That poor fucking girl!

The following week was a hard time for me, I'd never really done anything quite like that before, and didn't know what the repercussions would be. When I was out or at work I was constantly looking over my shoulder, and when I was at home I anxiously awaited that hard knock on the door from the police. I was terrified I'd go to jail for it. That was really something I didn't want to happen. Over the years I've drank on many occasions with men who had been in jail, and they all had the same dead look in their eyes. Like something important had been taken that could never be returned to them — not in this world anyway.

Several weeks passed and I completely forgot about the whole thing. I was back to my usual angers over working long hours for never enough pay, and the helplessness of my entire life — no, hopelessness, that's a better description.

I was at the gym one afternoon training with Charlie when my mobile phone rang. I was actually glad to hear it. He'd got a good takedown on me and was priming me for a choke.

"I have to answer the phone," I said.

"You're kidding man. You never answer when you're winning," said Charlie slowly letting go of my back in complete disgust.

"When do I ever win," I said smiling.

I got the phone out of my gym bag, accepted the call and held it to my ear. "Hello," I said and no one answered. I waited a few seconds and still no answer. As I was about to hang up I heard a slightly muffled voice begin to speak. "Listen you bastard. You nearly killed me the other night." Shit! I thought. I gave her my number. "You should be in jail right now. It's bastards like you that ruin women. Why did you do that stuff to me? I really liked you. You seemed a bit better than most the other guys." I didn't know what to say, what could I say? I just wanted to hang up, and get her out of my life. Problem was she had my number. After a long silence she spoke again. "Come round my place now and we'll have a talk," she said then hung up. I guess I had no choice now.

I got a shower and left the gym. I didn't tell Charlie what was happening—the less people that knew about this the better, I thought. I walked from the gym on Market Street to William Street. Walking up William Street was the easiest way to get to Kings Cross. It was the busy time of the day. There were lots of cars at a virtual standstill on the road—full of people desperate to get home and forget the day. The footpaths were crowded with hundreds of people in suits leaving offices and heading home or to bars, and the occasional fitness group jogging. My head was racing. What would become of all this? She really had me. I was totally trapped. Everything now was up to her. Thoughts and images rushed through my mind like a destructive whirlwind. I felt nauseous.

After what seemed like hours I arrived at her door. She opened it before I knocked. She must have been watching me through the peephole. I greeted her cautiously and she retreated to her sofa without responding. I followed her and sat as far away from her as I could. I fixed my eyes on the floor. I could see her looking straight at me from the corner of my eye. I didn't know what to do or say. As far as I was concerned there really was nothing to do or say. There was nothing between us at all. We weren't friends, and we definitely weren't lovers either.

It was getting quite uncomfortable in her lounge room. The atmosphere was so tense if I had a sledgehammer I could have smashed the air into thousands of tiny pieces. It was becoming ridiculous. We'd been sitting in silence for about 20 minutes now. Why was I even here if this was all she wanted to do? "Look Liz I am going. I really don't understand what the point of all this is," I said standing and heading for the door.

"Wait you bastard. You nearly killed me the other day, and that's all you have to say."

"What were you expecting? Why did you even call me?"

"I wanted to see you again."

"After I beat you up."

Liz went to the kitchen and came back with two glasses.

"You like American whiskey right?" she said handing me a glass.

I took it and drained it.

"Can I have that one too?" I said.

She handed me the other glass and I drained it in one long bitter swallow. It was strong stuff whatever she'd given me. Must have been 100-proof. It calmed me slightly. I let go of some of my anxiety. This wasn't so bad really. She wasn't so bad. She kind of looked like an angel with that lazy blonde hair and the white shirt she had on. "Look I am sorry. I am really sorry. If you want to get the law onto me, feel free. What I did was wrong," I said sincerely. She then hugged me and began crying on my chest. I really didn't know how to respond to this, this poor girl. We'd met at a bar and hit it off, ended up back at her place, I beat her up, and she didn't know what to do. I felt truly awful. I kissed her on the top of the head. "It will be alright. Everything will be alright," I said over and over. With the hope that if I said it enough, it would actually happen.

Before I knew it we were both naked on her bed. I was on my back and she was on top. What was the point of resisting anymore? If this was happening, it was happening. I may as well enjoy it.

She worked away for quite some time. It was pretty hot. She really had some special hip movements this one. She was making all sorts of noises. She was totally getting into it. I was interested, but I just couldn't really feel it enough to want to cum. After a while I felt myself going soft. It was really no fault of hers: I just couldn't do this with her right now, for whatever reason.

"That's it," I said.

"You came?"

"No."

She slowly got off me and gave me this strange look. It really annoyed me.

"What's wrong?" I said.

"Nothing," she said in a smartass sort of tone while standing up.

The way she said it made me angry. What the fuck did it matter to her anyway? If I didn't cum, I didn't cum.

"Hey fuck you!" I said.

She became furious. She lunged at me. I pushed her away. She landed hard on the floor. I got up and started getting dressed. As I was putting on my shirt she kicked me hard in the stomach. I was slightly winded. "Jesus! What did you do that for?" I said. She took a few steps back. Her eyes were blazing. She picked up a small gold Buddha off a shelf and threw it at me. It hit me right on the forehead. I suddenly saw a whole bunch of small lights dancing all over the room. It must have cut me: I could taste blood on my lips. She then grabbed hold of me. She held on desperately with all her strength. I head butted her and blood streamed from her nose. It looked like I had broken it. She stumbled back slightly dazed then lunged at me again—as if possessed by some unnatural force. She looked like an ancient warrior coming in for the kill. The expression on her face actually made me a bit nervous. I hit her with a hard right jab. She dropped to the floor without a sound. She was unconscious. I quickly left her place. My white shirt had blood all over it.

When I got to the street I took it off and threw it in a bin I noticed out the front of a convenience store.

Walking home the streets were as silent as I'd ever heard them. All I could hear was my pounding heart.

The next week I kept to myself, never leaving my apartment. I quit my job. It was time for a real change in my life, I'd decided. What I had been doing was just ridiculous. I couldn't keep on living like this. Police or no police, what was going on was not good. I stopped drinking. I barely slept. And when I did I just kept seeing her bloody face unconscious on the floor. And every time I did, I felt sick.

A few more days passed and I could feel myself changing. I could feel myself now yearning for something else: something different than anything I'd ever known. Was it possible? Who the fuck knows! But I was going to try: I was going to try my best.

I decided to start leaving my apartment again. I immediately went to the supermarket and got some groceries, and a bottle. I thought I deserved it.

When I got back to my apartment the door was open. Shit! I have been robbed, I thought. It really wasn't that unusual in my area. It boasts the highest concentration of junkies in the state. I had actually been pretty fortunate so far, I'd lived in the area for ten years and this would be the first time—not too bad. The thing was though: what if the thieves were still inside? I mentally accepted that they were. I put the shopping bags on the ground, cracked my knuckles, and slowly entered my apartment. It was night so there wasn't much light inside. Luckily I'd kept all the blinds open, so it wasn't pitch black or anything, you could still make everything out well enough thanks to the moonlight. I couldn't see anyone in the living room or kitchen. I then heard a bang in my bedroom, like something had been knocked off a shelf. Must be in there. Hopefully it's just the one. Will make things easier, I thought. I slowly moved to the closed door. I stood in front of it a few moments listening. I couldn't hear anything at all. They must have heard me. They couldn't have gone anywhere though: unless they jumped out of a two-story window. I kicked the door open and couldn't believe what I saw. It was Liz. She was drunk and standing at the end of my bed. She really didn't look well. "What the hell are you doing here?" I said turning on the light. She looked at me thoughtfully though didn't respond. I was actually a bit concerned. She was really out of it. She suddenly started crying. I didn't know what to do. I just kept my distance. Standing in silence observing her. I don't know how long it went on, I lost all sense of time, I couldn't seem to do anything though: it was as if I was trapped in a bad dream, with no control at all.

"So this is it is it? This is how you want it. You just want to dump me, like yesterdays garbage," she said angrily.

"I don't know what you mean Liz."

"Yea that's right: you and all the rest. None of you know what I mean. You are all cowards! I have needs you know."

"We all do."

"You bastard. I thought you were a real man. You've gone soft on me haven't you?"

"What I did was wrong."

"What would you know? Everything is wrong! Why change, nothing else does. The wrong never does—fuck you!" said Liz and began scratching at her face hard with both hands.

The short tough nails penetrated the skin leaving thin bloody trails running down her whole face. I winced at the sight of it. It was disgusting. It looked completely natural for her though, as if it was a regular action. She was getting really wound up and began letting out random screams. I stood there watching it being acted out like a play, that I didn't know my role in. "Well why don't you hit me now. Hit me NOW you bastard! Finish what you started: kill me! I don't want to live. I hate this fucking life. It's all a sham. It's all just bullshit. I don't want it anymore—just kill me, take me away from it!" she screamed while continuing to wound herself.

She soon became a bloody mess, she looked like a car had hit her or something; I had never seen anything like it before. Seeing her like this was terrifying to me.

Though it was all starting to make sense to me. She just wanted to die, I suddenly realised, coming out of the dream like state I was in. This whole time she just wanted to die. She went looking for guys she thought would do the job for her, because she couldn't do it herself. How many had there been? Surely it wasn't only me. There must have been more. She was so close to the truth she was unnatural for this world. She knew what she really felt and wanted—needed. She was like a divine figure. Like an angel: an angel of death, and everybody she touched was destined for the same path, if they played along that is. My whole life had been a never-ending series of loss and disappointment. That started as early as I could remember. Things were definitely bad for me, though I imagined they were for most others as well. It was different for her though; she had no place here, no place at all. Everything was just too clear to her, life was beyond bad for her: it was truly impossible.

I made the decision to leave her. I wasn't responsible for this. It was way beyond me. I turned around and left my apartment. I left everything I owned, and would never go back.

I could hear Liz screaming for several streets. Eventually her screams blended in with the sound of the night. As I walked along dark familiar streets, hoping to stumble upon something new.

THE LAST FIGHT

Billy "Beat Down" Henderson was once the most popular fighter in the world; that was a long time ago though. Now you would struggle to find a single fan: and that was how he liked it. He hated fans. He hated fighting too. But kept doing it because he had no other way to make money. He'd fight 2 or 3 times a year to earn enough to support his greedy ex-wife and brainwashed son: that he was never allowed to see, and live a basic life.

A few weeks earlier he got a call from Dino Night to replace Eddie Alvey in his welterweight title fight against Cam McDunn in less than three weeks time. He'd be fighting up a weight class and wouldn't need to cut weight for the fight. This was appealing to him. He wouldn't have to diet or train too hard.

McDunn was 27 and Irish and the new poster boy of the organisation. He had the whole of Ireland behind him and most of the world as well. He was the company's most popular fighter. He even had his first ever boxing match 7 months ago, that was as real as a pas de deux by the New York City Ballet, but still made over 100 million and gained even more fans.

Truth is Billy hated McDunn and everything he stood for. He'd love to smash that idiot's big mouth and soft face in with his trademark right hand, but wouldn't let that get in the way of his next check, and seriously doubted he could do it now anyway.

He was the company's bad guy: its most hated heel. They could sell the absolute shit out of this fight. And the rabbit they had in the hat was he had never been knocked out before. Dino Night had promised him a small fortune for this.

Billy had never thrown a fight. But there was a first time for everything. And he'd make enough from this one to give up fighting completely.

When he got the call for the fight he was at the end of a 4 day drinking session, which wasn't an uncommon thing for him now. He drank more than he trained. He hated training: what was the point anyway! The fans booed him win or lose. So why put any extra effort in, he often thought.

Billy always did the bare minimum these days in the gym, or didn't bother showing up at all. He cut ties years ago with his original trainer "Brains" Johnson; that took him in as a teenager and trained him all the way to the youngest-ever lightweight champion. Since then "Brains" has trained several champions but none ever had the same impact as Billy.

One of Night's conditions for the fight was he had to train with "Brains" again. Would make it look more authentic. Make the fuckers believe you could win this thing. Jesus! When you trained with him before you couldn't lose. I have never seen anything like it before, or since: it was beautiful, all those knockouts! No one will ever do that again. But don't get any funny ideas. If you win, or lose the fight in any way other than KO, the deal is off. And you will never fight in this, or any other smaller organisation again, I will see to that, he said to Billy in his office after he signed the fight contract.

A few hours and phone calls later he was training with "Brains" in a new gym that was nothing like the one they used to train in. It was really big and all the equipment was clean and new. He missed the old gym that was like a dungeon, with an old small ring somehow squeezed in there. There were no weights or treadmills or fancy machines, just sweat and impossible dreams.

He noticed his photo on the wall above all the other champions with a caption underneath saying: "BELIEVE!" He looked away from it quickly and didn't look at it again.

"Brains" ran him through a few minutes of pad work and he vomited. "Jesus! Let's watch some film instead. You been on that whiskey diet again," "Brains" said.

"Brains" knew nothing about the deal. He thought it was a real fight.

The training didn't go so well but "Brains" knew the talent inside his fighter could beat anyone given the right circumstance. Though he doubted this was the right circumstance.

The fight promotions were as expected. Everything McDunn said was greeted with applause and everything Billy said was greeted with hatred. He loved it. He remembered the line from that great French novel: "Hatred is the currency of the poor." All those fuckers are paupers, he thought.

Every night Billy would go to a bar on the other side of town. No one knew him there: that was how he liked it. He'd had fame and love. And those same people turned on him within moments when he lost a title fight. He had a broken right hand that he got in the first round but fought on for the next 4. He stopped using that arm for punching because of the pain and his opponent that was way below his level ended up getting an easy decision over him. No one knew about the broken hand other than "Brains" and he swore him to secrecy. That night everyone thought he threw the fight and started booing him and they haven't stopped since.

He began enjoying himself leading into fight week. The fans hatred was rich and potent and he loved that. The thing was, no matter how much they hated him, he would always hate them more: that was his ace.

The weigh-ins went easy. He ate a steak and fries a few hours before and still made weight. McDunn made weight as usual in his underwear then flexed his muscles and screamed like a retarded gorilla. Billy just stood there in a loose tracksuit laughing at him in the stare down. He had nothing to prove except losing and the massive payout.

That night he kept to his routine that saw him lose his last 5 fights, a bottle of whiskey and a hooker. It felt even better than it normally did, he never minded losing, he hated having to actually fight and the fear of doing something good in there that might make the crowd cheer for him. Though there would be no chance of that in this fight, and it would also be his last. Which made him happier than words could say.

He came faster than usually and told the hooker to leave. He turned on the television. There was an old clip of him knocking out Ramsey Downie the night he became the lightweight champ. He quickly turned off the television and looked at the walls.

Walking to the cage he was booed like never before—he loved it. He tried not to smile. If only I could tell these fuckers how much I hate them all. How their hero is nothing but an actor, and a bad one at that. That they are wasting their hard-earned money on a complete farce, he thought. He stopped walking a moment. A full cup of lemonade hit him in the head. He smiled.

He stood in the cage waiting for McDunn to come out. He was really taking his time. Billy didn't mind. Ready for a quick loss and the most money he had ever made.

"Brains" kept running him through the strategy. He nodded his head continuously but wasn't listening. All he could hear was McDunn's cheers. And they made him feel sick.

He was slightly hung over and hadn't slept much. He figured he could keep it going for 2 rounds and would let it go in the 3rd—had to make it look convincing: didn't want to risk any controversy that might jeopardize the payout.

McDunn finally made it to the cage and pranced around like a fool for a couple of minutes and the fight began.

Billy was immediately surprised by his lack of punching power. McDunn was meant to be a power puncher. It would be harder than he thought to make his punches look like they hurt him.

He'd never done anything like this before but it seemed to be going well. The crowd and commentators had completely fallen for his performance. He could even see Night in the front row smiling. And that bastard rarely smiled. This one was absolute money in the bank.

The second round finished and McDunn had landed 114 significant strikes to his 3. This was the round he would go down. He didn't want it to look too staged though.

He came out and threw a couple of punch combinations. One of the punches hit McDunn on the left cheek. It wasn't flush contact, but was contact none the less. The crowd collectively stopped breathing. McDunn wobbled a bit on his feet, and his facial expression went from cocky, to dazed. Billy looked at Night. He had a furious look on his face. He gave it a few seconds and McDunn was still dazed. If I hit him again this thing is over, he thought.

He shot for a takedown and lay on McDunn throwing the occasional weak hammer-fist so it looked authentic, hoping he would recover soon.

This went on for over a minute.

At that point something strange happened. The crowd started cheering louder than they had all night. Billy thought it was to wake up McDunn. Though they soon started chanting his name. He couldn't believe it; after all these years, after all their hatred: they were cheering him again. In a fight they all wanted him to lose. In a fight he didn't even train for or want to win. They were cheering. He thought about the early days. When he lived for the sport. When becoming a champion was everything to him. When he and "Brains" were inseparable. He looked out at Night. He now had the same smile he had earlier on his face. He could tell what he was thinking. He could tell what everyone was thinking. They wanted him to win. They wanted a new hero. They were all tired of McDunn. They wanted someone new to worship.

The fight was stood up. He felt a sudden burst of energy. He hadn't felt this for many years. That feeling like he was in a tight tunnel with nothing but him and his opponent in front of him, and a power inside that could tear anything to pieces. McDunn still hadn't properly recovered. He hit him with a few good body shots to soften him up. That was what he always did: go low then high. That was his secret.

For the next 30 seconds he landed more punches than he had in the last 5 years. McDunn was done: his left eye was completely closed and looked like he had nothing left. One more punch and the fight would be over.

Billy stopped and looked around the arena. All he could see was smiles. All he could hear was cheers. He thought about what winning this fight would mean to his life, then hit McDunn with the hardest body kick he ever threw.

McDunn was on all fours ready to be finished. Billy looked at the crowd again: their false smiles, their false cheers, their false heroes, their false lives: their false money they drown you in.

He hit McDunn with an illegal knee to the head. The fight was immediately stopped. McDunn won by disqualification. The crowd booed louder than he ever heard before. Night was furious.

Billy stood over McDunn smiling feeling completely free for the first time in as long as he could remember. The fight was over.

THE TRICK

Sweating on a Tuesday afternoon in my apartment in Sydney. Fish swimming through my mind, a jug of water and a bottle of whiskey staring me in the face, a small bag of coke in the bottom drawer. Looking at a copy of Chiron Review 101. It has 2 poems by me in it, along with Brautigan and some other good writers. The fan trying: but not strong enough to take away the heat. In an old apartment: always an old apartment. Though still fighting, not ready to hang up the gloves yet. Sometimes I think about it, then I go for a walk down the street or look at a newspaper or a television and it's there again—that endless need for words. Words to break down the walls, words to rain on the stupid fire, words to burn up the oceans of complete waste: this is the true purpose of the writer; to stand tall in a world of kneelers: to stay true to art.

I remember 14 years ago learning a trick that helped get me this far. At the time I was poor and starving and still finding the word. A regular job would have killed any chance I would have ever had of finding it.

I worked only 2 or 3 days a week maximum to get money for rent and a bag of rice: which really didn't go too far when I cooked it.

I ate boiled rice for breakfast, lunch, and dinner. I went from 95 to 70. I looked like a junkie. People would give me horrified looks when I passed them on the street: what they failed to see is they all looked far worse to me, with their childish hopes and dreams and lives. My main hope at the time was to simply not be like them! But getting back to the trick and point of this story. When you eat as little as I was it is very hard to sleep—it is very hard to do anything really. You are always hungry and feeling tired and disoriented. It is definitely tough, but without it, I would have never gotten where I needed.

My trick was to drink as much tap water as my stomach could possibly take after eating the boiled rice. Then lie on my side on the floor (that was my bed!) and push my knees as close as I could to my shoulders. Using the arms really helps get them nice and tight. And the tighter you get them, the fuller your stomach thinks it is. And make no mistake about it: without sleep you can't think, and if you can't think—you can't write.

I spent several years living like this: those years being some of the best and worst times of my life. Though without them, I wouldn't be writing this for you now. I wouldn't be writing at all. I would be just another lost face in the millions of lost faces that keep increasing by the day.

Brenton Booth lives in Sydney, Australia. He started writing when he was 19 and began sending the literary journals when he was 24. After nearly 10 years of rejections he had his first poem accepted for publication. Since then he has been published in over a hundred journals and anthologies internationally. He has been nominated twice for the Pushcart Prize and is the author of the chapbooks, *Dying Under an Unforgiving Sun, Dancing on the Cactus, Drowned as the Fish*, and the full length collection *Punching the Teeth From the Sky*, all available from Epic Rites Press.

www.ingramcontent.com/pod-product-compliance
Lightning Source LLC
Chambersburg PA
CBHW081459040426
42446CB00016B/3314